You Must have a Dream to have a Dream Come True!

How she teaches Mastermind Concepts through
Think and Grow Rich Success Principles

WORKBOOK

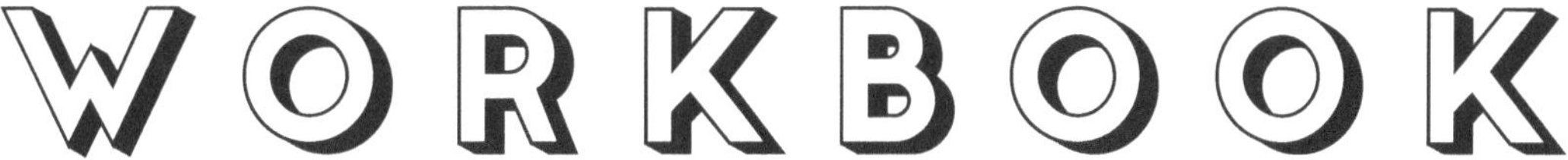

Ann McNeill

THE MASTER BUILDER

ISBN #: 979-8-88526-710-6

First Printing
February 2024

McNeill, Ann

Printed in the U.S.A.

Dear Masterminder,

Congratulations on taking greater steps towards unlocking your creative potential! This companion workbook is designed to be your practical guide, helping you transform the insights and principles from my book, 'You Must Have a Dream to Have a Dream Come True' into actionable, everyday practices.

What to Expect from This Workbook:

In the pages that follow, you will find a variety of exercises, activities, and reflections tailored to help you:

- Spark New Ideas: Through mind mapping and brainstorming techniques.

- Cultivate Daily Practices: With journaling prompts and mindfulness exercises.

- Embrace Risk and Experimentation: By stepping outside your comfort zone and trying new things.

- Enhance Your Professional Life: With strategies to integrate creativity into your life.

- Foster Personal Growth: Through engaging in diverse activities and lifelong learning.

How to Use This Workbook

This workbook is structured to be flexible. You can work through it from start to finish or pick and choose sections that resonate with you the most. Each activity is designed to stand alone, so you can tailor your creative journey to fit your unique needs and schedule.

Your Creative Future

As you embark on this journey, remember that creativity is a muscle that grows stronger with use. Embrace the process, be open to new experiences, and don't be afraid to make mistakes. Each step you take brings you closer to a more innovative, fulfilling, and dynamic life.

Thank you for choosing this workbook as your guide. I am excited to see where your creativity takes you!

Love,

Ann McNeill

iv

Contents

~ 1 ~
Spirituality

Spirituality involves cultivating a deep, personal relationship with God and putting Him first in all aspects of life. It means seeking to align one's actions, thoughts, and decisions with God's will, finding purpose through faith, and drawing strength and guidance from Him. This spiritual journey fosters inner peace, moral integrity, and a meaningful connection with the divine, ultimately guiding your life towards greater
fulfillment and purpose.

1. What are your top two goals in the area of spirituality?

Goal #1: ____

Action plan: ____

How often will you monitor this goal? ______________________

Goal #2: ____

Action plan: ____

How often will you monitor this goal? ______________________

On a scale of 1-10, where does your relationship stand with God in terms of daily prayer?

1   2 3 4 5 6 7 8 9 10

2. Explain how you arrived at that number. ______________________

____

____

3. Is prayer important to you? yes or no. Explain. ______________________

____

____

4. In what ways can you increase your prayer time with God on a daily basis? ______________

____

____

5. Do you read your Bible often? yes or no. If yes, how often do you read? ______________

____

____

6. If you do not read your Bible often, do you have a desire to start doing so? yes or no?
    Explain your answer. ____

____

____

7. Name three ways that you can begin to incorporate daily Bible study into your life.

        I.   ____

        II.   ____

        III.   ____

8. Why is it important to you to have mind, body, and spirit balance? ___________________

____

____

9. In what ways do you feed your spirit to keep it healthy? ______________________________

____

____

10. Is it important to you to go to church or the house of God? Explain___________________

____

____

11. Do you feel you need a stronger relationship with God? Explain. _______________

____

____

Forgiveness plays a big role in maintaining a healthy mind, spirit, and soul.

Forgiveness is the act of releasing someone for a wrong they did to you. Forgiveness is a reflection of God's grace since He is a God of forgiveness. God forgives us of our sins through Jesus Christ. In like manner, we must also forgive others when they have wronged us. Forgiveness promotes healing, reconciliation, and peace. True forgiveness involves a heartfelt decision to release the offender from their actions and putting it in God's hands and letting Him heal you.

Forgiveness also has to do with you asking for forgiveness from the wrong that you have done to others. Let' start with you and explore forgiveness in your life a little further.

12. If you found out that you only had a few weeks to live, who would you call to ask them to forgive you of a wrong that you did?

  i.   ____

  ii.   ____

  iii.   ____

13. On the lines below, write down the names of people who have wronged you, but you need to forgive.

  i.   ____

  ii.   ____

  iii.   ____

14. If you left a letter for someone to read after you died, who would that letter be written to? (write the name here: _____________________________. On the next page, write what you would say in that letter.   **TIPS:**

Be honest and sincere
Be heartfelt
Leave a lasting impression
End on a positive note

Letter to: _______________________________

From:___________________________   Date: _____________________

My Dream in the area of Spirituality 

~ 2 ~
Family

Family includes providing love, support, and guidance to each other, and creating a nurturing environment where members can grow and thrive. Family includes mutual respect, shared values, and commitment, and it plays a crucial role in shaping your identity and instilling values and traditions across generations. A family mission statement strengthens the bond between family members.

1. What are your top two goals in the area of family?

   Goal #1: ____

   Action plan: ____

   How often will you monitor this goal? ________________________________

   Goal #2: ____

   Action plan: ____

   How often will you monitor this goal? ________________________________

2. On a scale of 1-10, how strong is the bond between you and your immediate family members?

   1   2 3 4 5 6 7 8 9 10

3. Explain how you arrived at that number. ________________________________

____

____

____

In Ann McNeill's book, she quoted Stephen Covey when he defined a Family Mission Statement as the following: *"A family mission statement is a combined unified expression from all family members of what your family stands for, what it is that you really want to do and be as a family, and the principles you choose to govern your family life.*

*While considering the definition above, do you and your family have a Family Mission Statement? Yes or No? _______________ If no, would you be willing to work on one for your family? If yes, you must consult with each of your family members to ask them what is important to them as a family before writing the mission statement. You cannot write a Family Mission Statement without getting input from others in the family.

4. Write the names of each of your family members who will assist in helping to write the family's mission statement. Next to their names, write what they feel is most important in having a strong family unit. (You may use separate paper if necessary.)

Family Member Name: **What's Most Important to Them**

#1: _______________________   _________________________________

#2: _______________________   _________________________________

#3: _______________________   _________________________________

#4: _______________________   _________________________________

#5: _______________________   _________________________________

#6: _______________________   _________________________________

Example: The McNeill Family Mission Statement
*As a family, we are loving, peaceful, patient and kind to each other. Our generosity is shared with others as we live a life of significance while leaving a
family legacy.*

*Your Family Mission Statement can be shorter or longer.

5. On the lines below, write a draft of your Family Mission Statement.

____

____

____

____

Once your draft is completed, present it to every family member for their input, then work on it together until you come up with one that everyone agrees with.

6. If you already have a Family Mission Statement, answer the questions below:

- Do all of the family members know the Family Mission Statement?   Yes or No?

- Has everyone in the family memorized the Family Mission Statement?   Yes or No?

- Does everyone try to uphold the Family Mission Statement?   Yes or No?

- Is it time to revisit your Family Mission Statement?   Yes or No?

7. Do you mastermind with your family? Yes or No? If no, are you willing to start?

*If no, then the first thing that needs to be done is to introduce the mastermind concept to your family. You do not have to start with all of the categories at first. You may begin with spirituality, family, financial and education. You must be strategic with how to introduce the concept to the family. On the lines below, strategize exactly how you will present masterminding to your family.

Below is an example of how you can strategize:

1st: Explain to them about the importance of setting goals
2nd: Explain to them how to write 2-3 goals in different categories
3rd: Introduce the four categories to them (spirituality, family, financial and education)
4th: Give them ______ days to work on their goals with a meeting date to Return (you can decide how many days they need)
5th: On the meeting day, talk about the goals that they set and explain how to write action plans to accomplish them
6th: Set another meeting date to discuss the goals.

List your strategy for introducing the mastermind concept to your family below:

First: ____

Second: ____

Third: ____

Fourth: ____

Fifth: ____

8. In the chapter on 'Family' in Ann McNeill's book, she talked about 'Family Rituals.' Are there any family rituals that your family does to strengthen the family bond? List them below:

    i.   ____

    ii.   ____

    iii.   ____

9. How do those family rituals make you feel? ____

____

____

*Family Rituals are a wonderful way to strengthen the family bond.

REPAIRING FAMILY BONDS

10. Do you need to work on a relationship between you and a particular family member?

    i.   Who is that person? _______________________________

    ii.   What is their relationship to you? _______________________________

    iii.   How was the relationship between you and that person before the fragment?

____

____

____

iv.   What caused the relationship to fragment? _______________________________

____

____

v.   Are you willing to put the past behind you and embrace reconciliation?

____

____

vi.   What are you willing to do to take the first step towards repairing the fragment?

____

____

____

vii.   When will you start? ____

viii.   What do you think a positive outcome can be as a result of repairing the relationship?

____

____

____

ix.   Talk about forgiveness, the importance of it, and the beauty of reconciliation.

My Dream in the Area of Family:

~ 3 ~
Finances

Finances involve understanding and managing money through education and disciplined practices. It includes knowing how money works, how to multiply it, investing, saving, and spending it wisely. Financial success is built on clear goals, continuous learning, and self-discipline. Ann emphasizes the importance of having a detailed financial plan, seeking knowledge, and maintaining a balance between financial pursuits and personal values to achieve long-term financial stability and success.

1. What are your top two goals in the area of finances?

   Goal #1: ____

   Action plan: ____

   Goal #2: ____

   Action plan: ____

2. When do you plan on accomplishing these goals?

Goal #1:	**Goal #2:**
___ within 3 months	___ within 3 months
___ within 6 months	___ within 6 months
___ within 1 year	___ within 1 year
___ within 2 years	___ within 2 years
___ more than 2 years	___ more than 2 years

3. What do you plan to give in exchange for this money? _______________________

   ____

   ____

4. What frivolous spending do you need to cut out in order to develop a clear plan for reaching your financial goals?

     i. ___________________________________

     ii. _________________________________

     iii. ________________________________

5. Do you have a plan for retirement? __yes ___ no If yes, what is the plan(s)? If no, what is the plan to start one, and by when?

____

____

____

6. What investments have you made that will have a financial benefit to you 15 years from now?

     i. ___________________________________

     ii. _________________________________

     iii. ________________________________

7. If you are not able to identify any investments that will benefit you 15 years from now, are you willing to research and begin investing, even if you have to start small?

     _____ yes   _____ no

8. List the kind of investments that you can consider starting.

     i. ___________________________________

     ii. _________________________________

     iii. ________________________________

9. When would you like to begin your investment journey?

        ___ within 3 months
        ___ within 6 months
        ___ within 1 year
        ___ within 2 years

    *Write the month and the year here: ____

10. What is your action plan for getting started?

    i.   ____

    ii.   ____

    iii.   ____

11. What books will you read in the area of finance in order to educate yourself on financial literacy?

    iv.   ____

    v.   ____

    vi.   ____

12. When will you start reading the first book? ____

13. When do you plan on finishing that book? ____

Watch your Spending!

Often the things that we view in life as small purchases can make the difference between being financially comfortable and being broke. Once you calculate how much that morning bagel and cup of coffee really costs overtime, you will realize that making small, manageable changes in your everyday expenses can have just as big of an impact on your financial situation as getting a raise. Let's take a look at how much that morning bagel and cup of coffee really costs:

Bagel	$3.69
Coffee	$2.49
Subtotal	$5.18
Tax	$.37
Total	$6.55

Daily: $6.55

Weekly (5 days) $32.75

Monthly (20 days) $131.00

Yearly: $1,572

Cutting out that morning bagel and coffee and eating at home could put over $131 in your pocket a month and over $1,500 a year. These funds can go into your savings account.

My Dream in the area of Finances 

~ 4 ~

Education

Education is the process of acquiring knowledge, skills, values, and habits through formal instruction, personal study, and practical experience. It involves a lifelong journey of learning and growth, fostering intellectual development, critical thinking, and the ability to adapt to changing circumstances. Education empowers you to reach your full potential, contribute meaningfully to society, and pursue your personal and professional goals. Education is a vital tool for personal transformation and societal progress.

1. What are your top two goals in the area of education?

Goal #1: ____

Action plan: ____

How will you apply this goal to your life? ____

____

Goal #2: ____

Action plan: ____

How will you apply this goal to your life? ____

____

2. When do you plan on accomplishing these goals?

Goal #1:

___ within 3 months
___ within 6 months
___ within 1 year
___ within 2 years
___ more than 2 years

Goal #2:

___ within 3 months
___ within 6 months
___ within 1 year
___ within 2 years
___ more than 2 years

3. What are you doing right now to enhance you in the area of education? (reading a book, taking a class, learning a 2nd or 3rd language, learning something knew, etc.)

____

____

4. How is this enhancing you and contributing to your knowledge? ______________________

____

____

5. How will you apply this new knowledge (from question #3)? ________________________

____

____

6. What are you deliberately doing to continuously enhance yourself educationally? ________

____

____

7. What kind of specialized knowledge do you have? _______________________________

____

____

8. How can you use your specialized knowledge to take you to the next level? ____________

____

____

9. In what ways have you acquired self-education? In other words, how have you taken the initiative to learn something on your own, and what was it? ________________________

____

____

10. Do you share your knowledge with others? How do you do that? Explain. ________________

____

____

____

11. What steps are you taking to become the "go-to" person in your industry (or in the area of the thing that you love), and how do you assess your current level of expertise?

____

____

____

____

12. How do you apply the concept of specialized knowledge to your career, and what niche have you developed or are developing? ____

____

____

____

13. How do you balance formal education with self-education, and what role does each play in your lifelong learning journey? ____

____

____

____

My Dream in the area of Education

~ 5 ~

Personal Development

Personal development is the continuous process of self-improvement in knowledge, skills, habits, and character. It involves setting goals, enhancing self-awareness, and cultivating emotional intelligence to achieve a higher quality of life. By focusing on growth in areas such as mindset, discipline, and resilience, personal development empowers you to reach your full potential, overcome challenges, and lead fulfilling, purpose-driven lives. It is a lifelong journey of learning and self-discovery.

1. What are your top two goals in the area of personal development?

   Goal #1: ____

   Action plan: ____

   How will you apply this goal to your life? _______________________

   ____

   Goal #2: ____

   Action plan: ____

   How will you apply this goal to your life? _______________________

   ____

2. When do you plan on accomplishing these goals?

Goal #1:	**Goal #2:**
___ within 3 months	___ within 3 months
___ within 6 months	___ within 6 months
___ within 1 year	___ within 1 year
___ within 2 years	___ within 2 years
___ more than 2 years	___ more than 2 years

3. On the lines below, describe yourself in three adjectives. Don't think too hard about it. Just write the first three words that come to your mind. These are usually the most honest.

     i. ____

    ii. ____

   iii. ____

4. If someone were to ask you to tell them a little about yourself, what would you say? Write how you would describe yourself on the lines that follow:

____

____

____

____

____

____

5. Name three **unique** characteristics about yourself that sets you apart from others.

     i. ____

    ii. ____

   iii. ____

| **Strengths** | **Weaknesses** | **Opportunities** | **Threats** |

SWOT Analysis

A SWOT analysis evaluates Strengths, Weaknesses, Opportunities, and Threats for organizations, but it can also be used for personal development. A SWOT analysis helps identify internal strengths and weaknesses, as well as external opportunities and threats. It helps you to see your strengths, address weaknesses, seize opportunities, and mitigate threats, fostering growth and informed decision-making.

Directions: Complete the SWOT analysis below to identify areas of yourself.

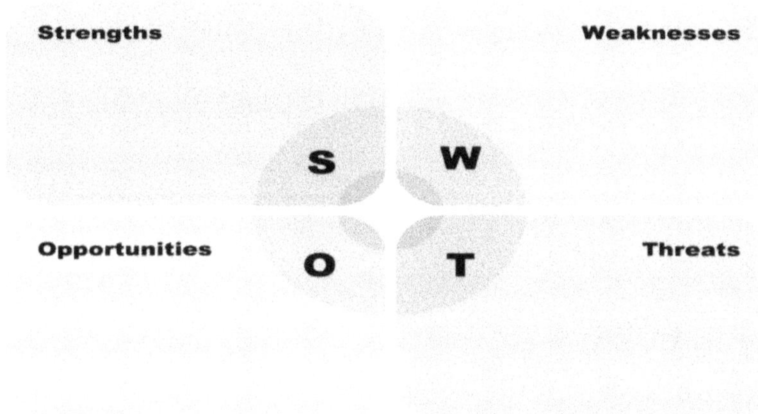

4. Write down three of your strengths.

      i. ____

      ii. ____

     iii. ____

5. How do you know that those are strengths?

____

____

____

6. Write down three of your weaknesses.

       i. ____

      ii. ____

     iii. ____

7. How do you plan on overcoming your weaknesses.

       i. ____

      ii. ____

     iii. ____

8. What opportunities can you capitalize on to elevate you in a particular area?

       i. ____

      ii. ____

     iii. ____

ANSWER THE FOLLOWING QUESTIONS USING THE RUBRIC BELOW:

5: Always   **4**: Almost Always   **3**: Sometimes   **2**: Almost Never   **1**:Never

1. I take time to write down the goals that I want to achieve. _______

2. I review my goals at least once per week. _______

3. I do something towards accomplishing my goals at least every week. _______

4. I take the time to meditate. _______

5. I spend time in prayer at least once weekly. _______

6. I feed my spirit by studying and reading the bible at least twice weekly. _______

7. I attend worship service at least twice monthly. _______

8. I take the time to read books to feed my mind and spirit. _______

9. I take a least one vacation per year. _______

10. I hang out with friends at least monthly. _______

11. I spend quality time with my family at least once each month. _______

<u>**5**</u>: Always   <u>**4**</u>: Almost Always   <u>**3**</u>: Sometimes   <u>**2**</u>: Almost Never   <u>**1**</u>:Never

12. My family and I eat dinner at the dinner table together. _______

13. I am content and satisfied on my current job. _______

14. I desire to change from my current position. _______

15. I make sure that I get adequate physical exercise at least twice weekly. ______

16. I make sure that I eat properly and manage my diet daily. _______

17. My bills are paid on time each month. _______

18. I am able to save money without touching it at least monthly. _______

19. I examine my thoughts daily to ensure that they are positive. _______

20. The mental attitude that I exhibit daily is pleasant. _______

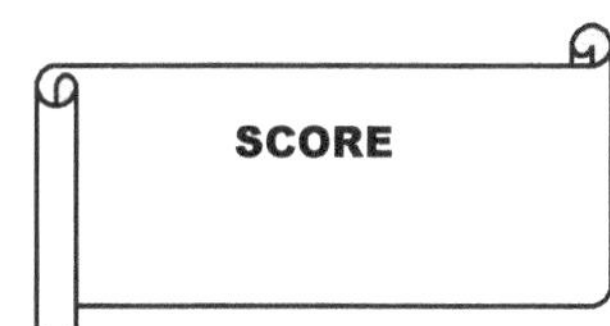

Add up your scores and refer to the results below:

81-100 (High) Congratulations! You are living your life to the fullest with balance, enjoyment, stability, and apparent joy! (May I hang with you?)

61-80 (Pretty High) Well done! You are making and taking time to live life with fulfillment and balance although there is a little room to add more.

41-60 (Average) It is good that you manage to keep your life maintained, but there is much room for improvement. Expand your consciousness.

21-40   (Low) Life is meant to be lived and you are not living it. You must begin to start living your life with purpose, meaning, and satisfaction.

Below 21 Now this is just sad. ☹

As you review your answers, look at the areas in which you have the lowest scores and decide how you plan on improving those areas. The rubric was created by asking questions in the following areas.

The first three questions dealt with **goal setting**.

The next four had to do with your **spiritual** life.

The next sentence dealt with feeding your **mind**.

The next four related to **family and recreation**.

The next one had to do with your **current job/career**.

The next two was **health**.

The next two was in the **financial** area.

The next two was your **mental attitude**.

9. My lowest scores were in: (Put a checkmark)

_____ Goal setting

_____ The spiritual area

_____ Family/recreation

_____ Job/career

_____ Health

_____ Financial

_____ Mental Attitude

I plan on doing the following to increase my actions in this/those areas:

____

____

____

____

10. Please write your goal and action plan for the area(s) that you scored a 1 or 2 in.

Area Needing Improvement: ____

Goal: ____

Action plan: ____

To be completed or increased by (Date)____

Area Needing Improvement: ____

Goal: ____

Action plan: ____

To be completed or increased by (Date)____

My Dream in the area of Personal Development

~ 6 ~
Health

Health is the state of physical, mental, and emotional well-being, not only the absence of disease or infirmity, but also maintaining a balanced lifestyle through proper nutrition, regular exercise, adequate rest, and mental care. Health is achieved by nurturing the body, mind, and spirit, enabling individuals to live energetic, resilient, and fulfilling lives. It also includes preventive measures, self-care practices, and a proactive approach to managing your overall wellness.

1. What are your top two goals in the area of health?

   Goal #1: ____

   Action plan: ____

   ____

   Goal #2: ____

   Action plan: ____

   ____

2. Do you exercise? ___ yes ___ no

   If yes, what kinds of exercise do you engage in? List them below:

   i. ____

   ii. ____

   iii. ____

3. How many times a week do you exercise?

_____ once a week	how may hours?	1 2 3 more
_____ twice a week	how may hours?	1 2 3 more
_____ three times a week	how may hours?	1 2 3 more
_____ more 3xs a week	how may hours?	1 2 3 more

4. Do you take vitamins or supplements? If yes, do you know what they do for your body?

Name of supplement: ____

What it does for your body: ____

Name of supplement: ____

What it does for your body: ____

Name of supplement: ____

What it does for your body? ____

5. Have you seen the following physicians in the last 12 months?

Primary care: ___ yes ___ no If no, why not? ________________________________

Optometrist: ___ yes ___ no If no, why not? ________________________________

Chiropractor: ___ yes ___ no If no, why not? ________________________________

Podiatrist: ___ yes ___ no If no, why not? ________________________________

Other: ___ yes ___ no ________________________________

Other: ___ yes ___ no ________________________________

Gynecologist (for women): ___ yes ___ no If no, why not? ________________________________

4b. If there were any areas of concern, did you follow up with you physician? ___ yes ___ no

If no, explain why not. ________________________________

6. When you are stressed out, how do you respond? ________________________________

____

____

7. Identify your top stressors and write strategies to manage and reduce them, such as meditation, exercise, or hobbies.

i. Stressor: ________________________________

Ways I can manage it: ________________________________

ii.   Stressor: ____

Ways I can manage it: ____

8. Does the way you manage stress help to improve your mental and physical health? Explain how?

____

____

9. Do you have a morning routine that includes things such as prayer, meditation, journaling, or exercise to set a positive tone for your day? If yes, list it/them below:

     i.   ____

     ii.   ____

     iii. ____

10. Select three healthy habits you want to develop (e.g., eating more vegetables, walking daily).

     i.   ____

     ii.   ____

     iii. ____

11. Did you drink enough water?   _____ yes   _____ no

12. What is your top goal in the area of health?

i.   ____

____

13. Why is this goal important to you?

i.   ____

____

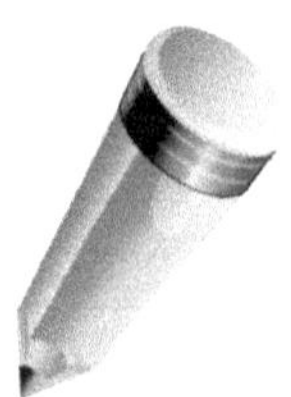

On the lines below, make your main goal is

SPECIFIC, **M**EASURABLE, **A**TTAINABLE, **R**EALISTIC and **T**IMEBOUND

S ____

____

M ____

____

A ____

____

R ____

____

T ____

____

Gratitude Journal:

Journalling is an excellent stress reliver and is a healthy outlet to express. For the next SIX days, write down what you are thankful for. You can do this in the morning, evening or at night.

Day 1: ________________________

Day 2: ____________________

Day 3: ____________________

Day 4: _______________________________

____

____

____

____

Day 5: _______________________________

____

____

____

____

Day 6: _______________________________

____

____

____

____

My Dream in the area of Health 

~ 7 ~

Business

Business is about creating and managing enterprises with strategic planning, innovation, and ethical practices. It involves resilience, adaptability, and a clear vision, aiming not only for profit but also for community contribution and economic growth. It's a continuous journey of learning and improvement, driven by a commitment to social responsibility and the betterment of society.

1. What are your top two goals in the area of business?

   Goal #1: ____

   Action plan: ____

   How will this goal take you to the next level? ______________________________

   ____

   Goal #2: ____

   Action plan: ____

   How will this goal take you to the next level? ______________________________

   ____

2. When do you plan on accomplishing these goals?

   Goal #1:   **Goal #2:**

   ___ within 3 months   ___ within 3 months
   ___ within 6 months   ___ within 6 months
   ___ within 1 year   ___ within 1 year
   ___ within 2 years   ___ within 2 years
   ___ more than 2 years   ___ more than 2 years

3. What business are you in? (This can be an official business or a business that you do on the side to make money. ____

4. What industry is your business in? ____

5. Do you have a solid business plan for the foundation for your business? ______________

____

____

____

6. Name the top three people, organizations, companies, or agencies, etc. that are at the top in your industry. (In other words, when you hear basketball, you think of Lebron James, when you hear of luxury cars, you think of Mercedes. When you hear the name of your industry, who is at the top and stands out as a leader in that industry?

    i. ____

    ii. ____

    iii. ____

7. What is it about them that makes them stand out as a leader in the field? ______________

____

____

____

8. What has been your successes and failures in this business?

SUCCESSES	FAILURES
______________________	______________________
______________________	______________________
______________________	______________________
______________________	______________________
______________________	______________________

9. Do you have mentors to guide and help you navigate pitfalls in the business? (If no, explain why not.)

____

____

____

10. Do you have a competitive advantage to help you stand out in your industry or your skill?

____

____

____

11. What is the most updated information or innovation that has happened in your field as of today? ____

____

12. Are you subscribed to any magazines or have joined any organizations that are affiliated with your field? ____

_______ yes   _______no

13. If no, are you willing to subscribe to a magazine or join an organization in your field? Explain. If yes, list the name of the magazine and /or organization(s) you are a part of.

____

Magazine: ______________________   Organization: ____________________

Magazine: ______________________   Organization: ____________________

Magazine: ______________________   Organization: ____________________

14. Are you active in any organization(s) in your industry? ___ yes ___ no

15. Do you have a position in the organization (i.e. secretary, treasurer, etc.)? ___ yes ___ no

16. If you are not active, would you consider becoming active in order to build relationships and garner more exposure to yourself? ___ yes ___ no

*If not, explain why not ____

____

If yes, what will you do to start becoming active? ____

____

17. Interview someone you know and respect who is successful in the same business that you are in and ask them the following questions.

INTERVIEW QUESTIONS:

(Write the answers on a separate sheet of paper)

- Why did you decide to go into this business?
- What do you like the most about this business?
- What makes you persevere in this business?
- How do you overcome bad days in the business?
- Do you think of ways to make you unique in this business (You don't have to reveal them to me.)"
- Is it important to know about current changes are innovations taking place in the field?
- What advice can you give me to help me be successful in this business?

My Dream in the area of Business 

~ 8 ~
Civics

Civics refers to the rights and duties of citizenship with an understanding of government functions at local, state, and national levels, and the active participation of citizens in shaping public policy and engaging in democratic processes. Civics involves being informed about current events, voting, attending public meetings, advocating for social justice, and joining impactful organizations.

1. What are your top two goals in the area of civics?

   Goal #1: ____

   Action plan: ____

   How does this goal help with community service? ____________________________________

   Goal #2: ____

   Action plan: ____

   How does this goal help with community service? ____________________________________

2. What city and state do you live in? ____

3. Without researching, do you know off hand the names of the following people? Put "Y" for (yes) or "N" for (no)

   __yes ___ no   your city mayor

   __yes ___ no   your city commissioners

   __yes ___ no   the county mayor

   __yes ___ no   the county commissioners

   __yes ___ no   your state representative

   __yes ___ no   your state senator

   __yes ___ no   your two congress people

4. If you did not know the names of those people from the previous page, research who they are and write their names on the lines below:

        your city mayor ____

        the vice city mayor ____

        the county mayor ____

        your state representative ____

        your state senator ____

        your two-congress people ____

5. Which one of them (above) are you willing to get to know in order to keep up with what is going on from a city, county, state or national standpoint?

Name:______________________________   Position:______________________________

Email address:____________________   Phone #: ______________________________

Topic of discussion: ____

6. Have you attended any of the following within the last year?

        _______ a city commission meeting

        _______ a county commission meeting

        _______ other civic affiliated meeting/conference

7. Are you familiar with the current voting laws in your state and how it may impact you or your family?   _______ yes   _______ No

8. Rate your current level of civic engagement from 1-5 with 5 being the strongest in the areas below:

        _____ voting

        _____ attending public meetings

        _____ participating in community services

        _____ is a member of a civic organization

        _____ have an understanding advocacy

        _____ have an understanding of public policy

9. On the lines below, research the current voting laws in your state, what the changes are and how they may affect you or someone you know.

____

____

____

10. How can joining civic and professional organizations impact your community involvement and career? ____

____

____

____

11. Why is it important to understand how the government functions at local, state, and national levels? ____

____

____

____

12. Do you know the history of the following ("Y" for yes, "N" for no)?

______ your state   ______ your city   ______ your county

13. What modern day civic leader do you know of offhand? If you cannot think of anyone, research someone and give some information about them in the lines below:

____

____

____

____

My Dream in the area of Civics

~ 9 ~
Recreation

Recreation is essential for achieving a balanced and fulfilling life. It involves engaging in activities for enjoyment, relaxation, and pleasure, providing a necessary break from daily routines and responsibilities. Recreation reduces stress, improves mood, and enhances overall well-being. It creates lasting memories, promotes mental rejuvenation, and offers opportunities for personal growth and exposure to new experiences. Prioritizing recreation helps maintain mental health and enriches life in ways that work alone cannot provide.

1. What are your top two goals in the area of recreation?

   Goal #1: ____

   Action plan: ____

   How does this goal help with community service? ___________________

   Goal #2: ____

   Action plan: ____

2. When do you plan on accomplishing these goals?

   Goal #1:   **Goal #2:**

   ___ within 3 months   ___ within 3 months
   ___ within 6 months   ___ within 6 months
   ___ within 1 year   ___ within 1 year
   ___ within 2 years   ___ within 2 years
   ___ more than 2 years   ___ more than 2 years

3. Why is recreation essential for maintaining mental health and achieving balance in life?

   ____

   ____

4. How did Ann McNeill's experiences with her grandson demonstrate the importance of making and keeping promises?

____

____

____

5. What impact did Ann McNeill's trip to Africa have on her and her daughter's perceptions and understanding of different cultures?

____

____

____

6. Why is traveling and exploring different parts of the world important?

____

____

____

7. How can exposure to diverse recreational experiences expand a child's mind and influence their future aspirations?

____

____

____

8. Why is it important to intentionally plan and prioritize recreational activities in a busy

schedule? ____

____

____

9. How can making time for recreation prevent a life filled with regrets and missed opportunities for joy and relaxation? _______________________________________

____

____

10. Are you able to schedule a family day within the next 30 days for an activity that will promote bonding and relaxation.

Day: _______________________________   Date: _______________________________

Title of this Family Day: ____

Location for Family Day: ____

Things to be done on this day:

 i. ____

 ii. ____

 iii. ____

Family Members expected to be there:

1._______________________ 4._______________________ 7._______________________

2._______________________ 5._______________________ 8._______________________

3._______________________ 6._______________________ 9._______________________

11. On the lines below, write three things that you can do or places you can go to have a good time and bring laughter and joy into your life.

 i. ____

 ii. ____

 iii. ____

 iv. ____

12. Who are the people that you would share this pleasurable time with?

     1.____ 4. .____

     2.____ 5. .____

     3.____ 6. .____

13. Why did you choose the (above) people to share this recreation time with?

____

____

14. What is stopping you from doing this within the next three months?

____

____

15. On a scale of 1-10, how likely are you in the very near future to do some, if not all the things you listed?   1 2 3 4 5 6 7 8 9 10

On the lines below write down some things that you would like to do.

Within the next 12 months:

I would like to: ____

Targeted Month/Year: ____

Reason why you want to do this: ____

____

Travel Plans

I would like to travel to: ____

When would you like to go? ____

With Whom? ____

For how long? ____

How will you prepare for this trip? ____

Write down some things you would like to do in the years to come.

Within the next five years

I would like to ____

Targeted Month/Year: ____

Reason why you want to do this: ______________________________________

____

Travel Plans

I would like to travel to ____

When would you like to go? ____

With Whom? ____

For how long? ____

How will you prepare for this trip? __________________________________

Within the next ten years:

I would like to ____

Targeted Month/Year: ____

Reason why you want to do this: ______________________________________

____

Travel Plans

I would like to travel to: ____

When would you like to go? ____

With Whom? ____

For how long? ____

How will you prepare for this trip? __________________________________

Within the next twenty years:

I would like to ____

Targeted Month/Year: ____

Reason why you want to do this: ____

____

Travel Plans

I would like to travel to: ____

When would you like to go? ____

With Whom? ____

For how long? ____

How will you prepare for this trip? ______________________________________

Below is a list of some additional things you can do for recreation and relaxation:

1. indoor family games
2. outdoor games
3. line dancing
4. cell phone games
5. drawing
6. recreational reading
7. going to the beach
8. movie night
9. watching a movie

My Dream in the area of Recreation

~10~
Creativity

Creativity is the ability to generate new and original ideas, solutions, or approaches by thinking outside the box. It involves embracing new experiences, experimenting with different perspectives, and continuously learning. Cultivating creativity includes exploring curiosity, practicing mindfulness, engaging in diverse activities, and taking risks.

1. What are your top two goals in the area of creativity?

   Goal #1: ____

   Action plan: ____

   Goal #2: ____

   Action plan: ____

2. Why is meditation important for enhancing creativity, and how can you practice it?

   ____

   ____

   ____

3. What are the benefits of engaging in new and diverse activities for your creative process?

   ____

   ____

   ____

4. How does taking risks contribute to developing creativity, and how can you overcome the fear of failure? ____

____

____

5. How can you leverage your unique perspectives and talents to set yourself apart creatively in your personal and professional life? _______________________

____

____

6. How can you effectively build your personal brand and keep your brand strong?

____

____

7. As it relates to your gift, your position, or what you love to do, list some ways that you can be creative and do what you do differently and creatively.

    i. ____

    ii. ____

    iii. ____

8. What kind of outcome do you think can happen as a result of you doing things more creatively? ____

____

____

____

Money Circles

Using creativity can help you identify other areas of your life where you can bring supplemental income to you. Money circles help you identify different ways in which you may bring income into your life through your God-given talents. In the center of the circle, write your primary source of income. In the outer circles, write other ways that you can make money. Then, you must make the time to pursue those other areas in order to bring additional cash flow into your life.

Take a look at the money circles below. Use them to see how you can identify areas that will benefit you in a monetary way.

Money Circle Example:

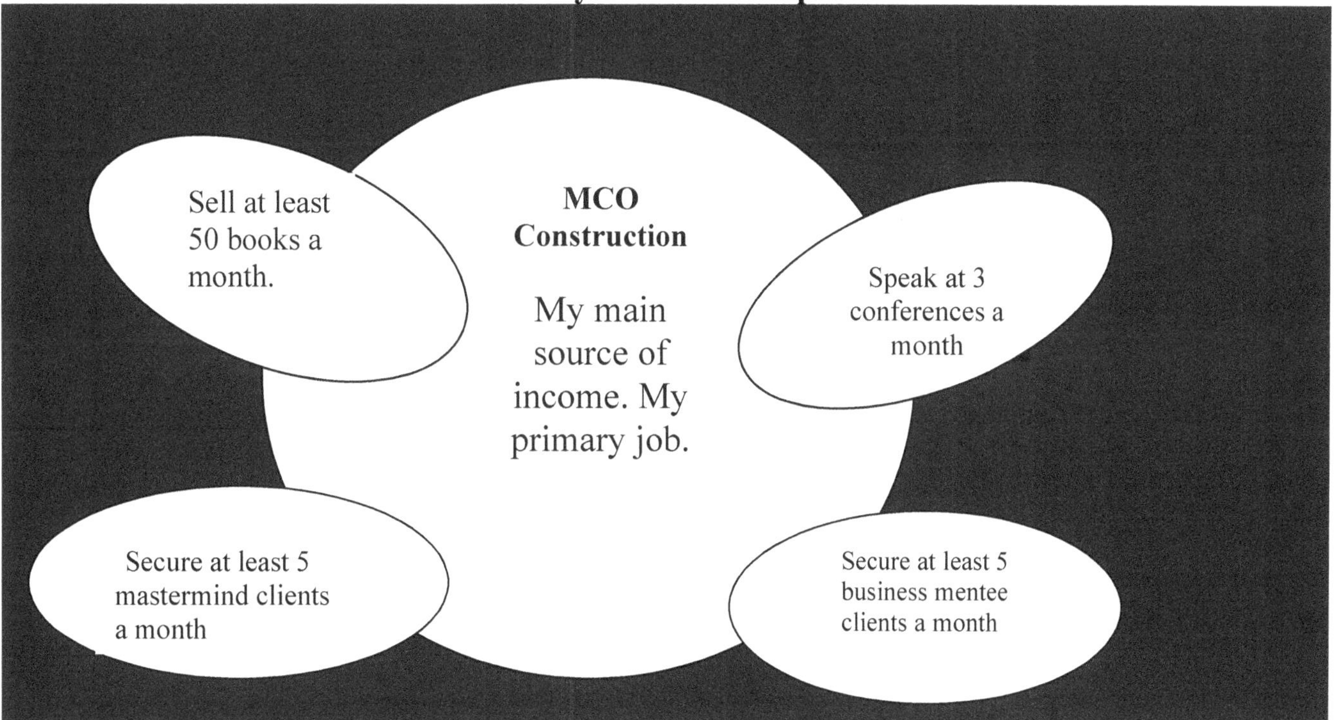

Fill in your money circles below:

On the lines below, take an inventory of yourself in order to recognize your creative potential.

THINGS THAT ARE GREAT ABOUT ME:
On the lines below, list the great things about yourself that most people don't know about you.

i. ____

ii. ____

iii. ____

THINGS I KNOW:
On the lines below, list some things that you have knowledge of. This is what the *average person* does not have knowledge of.

i. ____

ii. ____

iii. ____

THINGS I CAN DO:
On the lines below, list some things that you can do that the *average person* cannot do.

i. ____

ii. ____

iii. ____

THINGS I OWN:
On the lines below, list things that you own that the *average person* does not own.

i. ____

ii. ____

iii. ____

PEOPLE I KNOW:
On the lines below, list the names of people you know or have met, that the *average person* has not.

i. ____

ii. ____

iii. ____

JOBS I HAVE HAD:
On the lines below, list the jobs you have had that the *average person* has not had.

i. ____

ii. ____

iii. ____

THINGS I HAVE DONE:
On the lines below, list things that you have done that the *average person* probably has not done.

i. ____

ii. ____

iii. ____

THINGS I AM SENSTIVE ABOUT:
Here you are to list the great things that make you emotional, bring tears to your eyes, or cause you to become vulnerable or afraid.

i. ____

ii. ____

iii. ____

> This exercise should have enlightened you. As you look back over your list, you should be amazed at the things that you are discovered about yourself. That information contributes to the person you are. You have experienced a lot and oftentimes we don't reflect on all the things we know, have, heard, or seen. If you don't think that your list is impressive, then as long as you wake up each day with your health and strength, you can change what and how you do things each day. You are the master of your destiny.
> You are the captain of your ship.

Below is a list of other things you can do to enhance your creativity.

- ✓ **Journaling**: Keep a daily journal to express your thoughts, experiences, and creative ideas.
- ✓ **Meditation**: Practice mindfulness meditation to clear your mind and enhance your focus.
- ✓ **Art Projects**: Engage in painting, drawing, or sculpting to express yourself artistically.
- ✓ **Learn a New Skill**: Take up a new hobby or skill, such as playing a musical instrument or learning a new language.
- ✓ **Experiment with Photography**: Take photos from different angles and perspectives to see the world in new ways.
- ✓ **Daily Sketching**: Draw something every day, no matter how simple, to keep your creative muscles active.

My Dream in the area of Creativity

Ann McNeill

Ann McNeill is President/CEO of one of South Florida's few African American-female owned construction companies. McNeill Construction (MCO) was founded 40 years ago and is still one of the leading minority firms in South Florida in the area of construction management and project controls. MCO construction has worked on the majority of the flagship projects in South Florida, such as The Miami Airlines Arena, The Marlins Ballpark, The Miami International Airport, The Miami Science Museum, The Miami Children's Courthouse and many more.

As a female licensed general contractor, Ann discovered that women in the construction business were far and few between. She strongly believed that a network of women in construction needed to be created. As a result, Ann started The National Association of Black Women in Construction (NABWIC). The association was created to help build a pipeline for black women in the public sector, black women in the private sector, black women entrepreneurs and young ladies in school. The main purpose of NABWIC is to create a network of professional women in the construction industry who teach each other how to turn contacts into contracts. This is done through a "Billion Dollar Luncheon", which is held each month. As a result of her track record of accomplishments, Ann has been featured in Black Enterprise Magazine, USA Today and ABC's World News.

She is also President of MCO Consulting, Inc., a consulting company that provides outreach, monitoring and compliance for private sector firms that work on public sector land. She has received numerous awards and recognitions for her work in her industry and also in the community. She received her Bachelor's Degree in accounting from Florida Memorial College (University) and her Master's Degree in finance from Barry University. She is married to Daniel McNeill and has two daughters, Danelle and Ionnie. She also has one grandson, Malachi and a granddaughter, Rajahnia.

www.ingramcontent.com/pod-product-compliance
Lightning Source LLC
Chambersburg PA
CBHW041815110726
48006CB00019B/2391